Little Steps
for
New Parents

What people are saying about
Little Steps for New Parents:

What a terrific book! The idea of giving parents bits of useful information on a weekly basis is simply brilliant. And I loved the layout—especially all those pictures of dads and babies.

Wade F. Horn, Ph.D. President, The National Fatherhood Initiative

As a grandmother of six, I have found your book a tremendous help for each of my four daughters and their first encounter with their newborns. The easy way it is laid out meant they didn't have to look through pages of information. Keeping the journal was fun too.

Barbara Eldridge, President Mindmasters

The simplicity, quality of information, and opportunity to actively enjoy being a family right from the beginning make this journal something to use and then treasure for a lifetime.

Carol Kuna, M.A. Early Childhood Specialist

As more is learned regarding the importance of infant brain development and stimulation, parents will become increasingly eager for suggestions on how to provide a suitable environment for their infant. *Little Steps for New Parents* is a great tool.

Parent Educator and Program Specialist, FL.

From a special group of young mothers in Long Beach, CA:

I love writing about my baby. This is a whole year's worth of treasured memories.

This book helps me understand more about my baby and the different things I can do.

This book gives me encouragement to do my best as a mother and tells me things to do for myself and my baby and I feel more confident.

This book explains how much love and attention my baby needs and it really helps me to learn how to communicate with my baby.

I learned that it is important to make my baby feel comfortable, loved, safe, and secure. When he grows up I will show him the book.

Little Steps
for
New Parents

Birth to One Year

A Weekly Guide for Developing

Your Baby's Intelligence

Sandy Briggs

PERSONHOOD PRESS
!!!Books for ALL that you are!!!

Little Steps for New Parents: Birth to One Year
A Weekly Guide for Developing Your Baby's Intelligence
by Sandy Briggs

Consultants: Carol Kuna Lapetito, M.A. Early Childhood Special Education
Nancy B. Carlson, Ph.D., CCC/SLP Speech Pathologist
Susan Bañuelos Smith, R.D.

Editor: Gail M. Kearns
Book Production: Penelope C. Paine
Layout & Typography: Christine Nolt, Cirrus Design
Cover Design: Robert Howard

(800) 662-9662
E-mail: personhoodpress@att.net
Web Site: http://www.personhoodpress.com

Every effort has been made to present the most accurate and accepted developmental practices. However, each baby has different needs, and this information may not be appropriate in every case. We urge that you check with your physician, midwife, or other related health professionals before undertaking or choosing not to undertake any course of action, and we recommend that you always follow the advice and recommendations of your health practitioner. Sandy Briggs is not a medical professional, nor is she engaged in rendering medical advice. She takes no responsibility for any consequence relating directly or indirectly to any information, recommendation, treatment, procedure, action or application of medicine by any person using this book.

Library of Congress Catalog Card

ISBN L-932181-04-0

Contents

You are your baby's first and most important teacher. And, yes, you are qualified for this critical position. There is no such thing as a perfect parent—you simply do your best. For healthy development, your baby needs to be loved, talked to, held, and allowed to explore. It's likely that not having enough time will be your biggest challenge. Make being with your baby your first priority.

Introduction

Scientists now know that the very first years of life are critically important for healthy brain development. The environment you provide, especially in the first three years, has a profound effect on that development and your baby's future.

Because of this, *Little Steps* is somewhat different than other books you may have read on child development. The main focus is the development of your child's brain.

The many simple and enjoyable activities included here will help your baby's development in the early years. We also give you information to help you better understand how your child is developing. This understanding will help guide you in the upcoming years.

A loving and interesting environment will have a positive impact on your baby's future. Neglect and or being exposed to constant anger or stress will have a negative impact on your child's future.

Much of the foundation for your baby's future is being built in the first three years of life. These three years will, to a large degree, determine how well a child will:

- Learn
- Solve problems
- Express and control emotions
- Get along with others
- Form their attitude toward life

Fortunately, babies are very motivated to learn. They are curious and want to touch everything. They look for the chance to build their skills (and their brain). They will repeat and build upon a skill until they are ready to move on to the next step.

The good news is that the more enjoyable you make this time for you and your baby, the better the chance your child has of becoming a confident and competent adult.

Playing is one of the best ways for you to help your child develop. Simple play like trying to hold or grab a rattle is important brainwork for your baby. So is seeing you smile. Even touching your face is a learning experience.

Knowing that you are there when she needs you is one of the most important things you can do for your baby. She quickly learns that she's safe to explore and learn when you are there just in case she needs help. This helps her build confidence.

There's no reason to pressure your baby into learning something that she's not ready for or doesn't want to do—at least not at this age. We all learn best when we're having fun, enjoying ourselves, and when something is interesting.

It's a challenge for you to provide interesting activities and yet not pressure your baby to move at too fast a pace for her. Don't worry—you'll do just fine. Your baby will give you lots of clues. You'll find that you quickly become creative and patient.

Your baby is an individual with her own special talents and personality. Treasure these and help her develop into the very unique person that she is. This does not take expensive toys. It does take love, time, patience, and lots of hugs.

WE CONTINUE TO LEARN ALL THROUGH LIFE, BUT IT SEEMS THAT THE EARLY YEARS SET THE STAGE.

A Special Message

One of the most frustrating challenges for a parent or a caregiver is how to deal with a crying baby. Sometimes a baby's needs are obvious and quickly taken care of. Sometimes you simply have no idea how to help.

Some of the most common reasons for crying are hunger, discomfort, or just being tired. Sometimes your baby really needs to be picked up and held, and sometimes he just wants to fuss. If your baby seems to be in pain, call a doctor.

Infants and young children need to be held and touched. Their brains need input and stimulation to develop, and they are eager to gain new information. By crying, they get this needed attention and food for their brains.

If feeding and changing your baby doesn't work, try waiting for a few minutes. Pat him on the back and quietly talk or sing. Place his thumb in his mouth. (Babies comfort themselves by sucking their thumb or a pacifier.) Hold him to your chest and walk around, and hold his feet so that he feels secure. Go for a walk in the stroller. Go for a ride in the car. Rocking chairs often work and are comforting for both you and your baby. Turning on the vacuum cleaner seems to quiet some babies.

Research shows that the best thing to do is to pick up your baby when he cries. In the first year, he will not become spoiled. In the long run, he'll learn faster how to calm himself—he doesn't know how to do this yet. Babies that are picked up soon after they start to cry seem to cry for shorter periods of time.

Babies cry often in the first two to three months of life and then this gradually declines. Some do cry more (and longer) than others. Many still believe that you should just "let them cry it out." Even as tired as you are, it is best to pick up your baby.

In later months, babies can become frustrated and get fussy when a new skill (or toy) is just out of reach. If this is the case, step back and wait a few minutes. Let your baby try for a while before you help.

Sometimes there is nothing you can do. Your baby is not crying to upset you. Many parents feel helpless, and some begin to feel angry. Some anger is normal, but if your anger begins to get out of control, put your baby in a safe place and leave the room until you cool off. It's far better for your baby to continue to cry than for you to get physically violent.

NEVER SHAKE YOUR BABY. Brain injury, blindness, or even death can occur. Never leave your baby with anyone who cannot control his or her anger.

How to Use This Book

Each week spend a few minutes reading the activity and notes. Write your own notes in the space provided. Writing down what you and your baby are doing will help you understand your baby. And you'll enjoy reading and sharing this journal in later years.

Review past weeks often, and continue to use the activities as long as your baby enjoys them. Babies love repetition. It's one of the ways they build their brains.

Dads too will find that these activities are a great way to become close to his baby right away.

For parents who have infants with special needs, talk with your health professionals and Early Intervention Specialist to guide you in the best ways to get the most out of these activities.

Your baby will develop at his own pace. Don't be disappointed if he's not ready for an activity we have suggested. Not all activities will appeal to your baby. Follow his lead—he knows what he likes and when he is ready!

In the first years as genes and experiences blend to form a unique personality, the foundation for the future is being laid.

Baby's Name _____

Date of Birth _____

Time of Birth _____

Hospital _____

City_____ State _____

Notes _____

_____

_____

First Things First—Bringing Baby Home

Every new parent feels a bit overwhelmed when they first come home with their tiny, fragile little bundle. Even people who have spent a lot of time with infants are somewhat anxious when they first bring their own baby home. The important thing right now is to make your baby feel comfortable, loved, safe, and secure.

Pick up your baby when she cries, and try to find out what she needs. It may be hugging and cuddling. Picking up a newborn each time she cries will not spoil her. It's important for her to learn that you will take care of her needs and that she is safe. When she is picked up often at an early age, it's more likely that she will begin to learn how to calm and quiet herself at an earlier age.

Feed your baby when she's hungry. At first, she may want to eat every one to two hours.

Talk and smile. Your baby can see your face, smell you, feel your skin, hear you, and can even sense how you feel.

Health and Safety

Put your baby on her back when she sleeps. Make sure she's on a firm surface with no pillows or stuffed animals. Your baby needs to be able to easily move her head to breathe.

Keep your baby away from cigarette smoke. It's very harmful to growing lungs.

Breast milk is the best food for your baby. Breastfeeding is new for both of you, and many moms need a little help. Don't hesitate to ask for it!

Never shake your baby. This can easily cause brain damage and even death.

Choose babysitters very carefully. Don't choose people who are easily upset or violent. Find someone who has lots of time to cuddle your baby.

Loving care helps your baby's physical and mental growth. Neglecting your baby is both a physical and mental health risk.

Always read the information you receive from your health professional about your baby's health and well being. Ask questions even if you think they may sound silly. It's important for you to understand your baby's needs.

You need to be healthy too. Eat nutritious foods and drink plenty of fluids. Take only the drugs prescribed for you by your doctor. Rest or take a nap when your baby is sleeping.

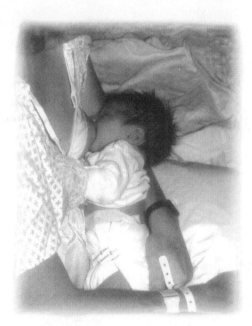

Always put your baby in the car seat when riding in a car. Car seats save lives but most are not used or installed properly, or don't fit the car. Learn how to protect your baby.

Week 1

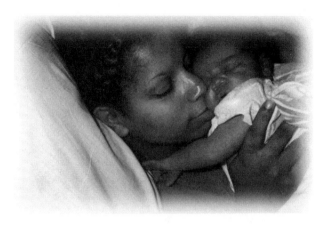

As you begin this exciting journey filled with loving, laughing, and crying, you are probably experiencing many emotions and have many concerns. Don't worry. Mother Nature did a good job in preparing mothers, fathers, and even babies for this adventure. You may have doubts about this now, but you will gain confidence.

Getting to know each other can take a little time. When your baby is awake, cuddle and talk to him. He needs lots of love.

It's likely that your baby is going to want to eat about every two hours—both day and night, for awhile. Feed him when he's hungry. In between feedings, lay down and relax.

If your baby cries, pick him up and feed him, change him, or try to calm him. Picking up your baby when he cries will not spoil him. Let your baby establish his own feeding schedule.

Health

Baby: Be careful. Babies' heads and necks are fragile. Always support the back of his neck and his head when you pick him up.

Mom: Many new mothers have "the baby blues" right after birth. Disappointment, sadness, crying, feeling tired, and worrying about being able to handle all of this is pretty normal. Overwhelmed is a word that often describes new moms.

Feeding

After your baby is several days old, make sure he wets six or more diapers a day. This will let you know if he's is eating enough. Don't let him sleep more than five hours at a time before feeding. If he falls asleep and you don't think he's eaten enough, gently wake him.

Keep a list of questions to ask your doctor. Don't forget YOUR health, too.

My Thoughts . . .   Date

_____

_____

_____

_____

_____

_____

_____

_____

_____

_____

_____

Your baby is already beginning to learn about his world. When he's awake and alert, he's learning about this big, new world. He'll enjoy gazing into your eyes. Your smile and talking are already stimulating brain growth.

17

Week 2

Baby talk is a natural way for parents to talk to their baby. Don't worry about sounding silly. Your baby will enjoy it, and it provides just the type of sounds she needs. You'll notice that most people will talk baby talk to your baby.

Your baby's eyesight will take awhile to develop. Right now, your baby can see things that are about 8 to 10 inches away (about the distance from her face to yours when you are feeding her). Things that are farther away are fuzzy.

Put your face close to your baby's face and smile and talk to her. You can start by saying anything. See how she watches and listens to you. Babies love to look at faces and listen to voices.

Tell her that you're going to pick her up and feed her. Tell her all the things you are seeing as you take a walk. Tell her how wonderful she is and how much you love her. Sing to your baby. She really likes to hear the sound of your voice and won't mind if you're not a good singer.

Health

It's time for the doctor to see your baby for a two-week checkup. Bring a list of any questions you have.

Carry your baby as much as possible rather than put her in a stroller. She's getting a lot more "brain stimulation" when she's being held.

My Thoughts . . .   Date

_____

_____

_____

_____

_____

_____

_____

_____

_____

_____

Did you know that your baby is already learning how to talk?
Every time you talk to her, her brain stores sounds that will
one day be words. She learns to talk by listening to you and
other important caretakers in her life.

Week 3

Cuddle and hold your baby often. This is good for his development in many different ways. It's especially important in the first years.

One way to have your baby close to you is with an infant carrier that holds him securely on your chest. Your baby can hear your heartbeat and feel your warmth. Plus, he will be close enough to see your face and hear you talk.

Dads are often concerned about how to pick up and hold this tiny baby. But it's important for your baby's healthy development for Dad to be involved. The sooner, the better. (Grandpas, uncles, and caring friends are good, too.)

Have Dad sit in a comfortable chair. Gently place the baby in his arms so that the baby's head and neck are well supported. Show Dad how to put his face close and talk to him.

Health

Keep your baby away from cigarette smoke. Secondhand smoke is not good for adults, and is especially harmful for little babies.

Health

Diarrhea can be a very serious problem for babies if not treated. Continue to feed your baby. If he won't take food, or if the diarrhea lasts more than 8 hours, call your doctor. Call the doctor immediately if your baby has blood in his diaper.

Learning how to talk is an amazing mental accomplishment. Much of the foundation for this learning is built before age one.

My Thoughts . . .   Date

_____

_____

_____

_____

_____

_____

_____

_____

_____

_____

Your baby's brain is getting information from everything that he hears, sees, smells, touches, and tastes. Even though he's only awake for short periods of time, there's a lot of brain building going on. He gets the kind of information his brain needs when you hold him and talk to him.

Week 4

You'll be amazed by how much your baby will grow this year. Using washable finger paints, make a handprint and a footprint on the next page (or use one of the blank pages in the back of the book). Do this several times during the year.

Bath time is a good time for you and your baby to grow closer. She will begin to associate you with comfort and pleasure. It will probably be a little awkward at first, for both of you. It can be difficult to support your baby's head and neck and still bathe her.

Playing in the bath is a perfect place to learn many new things. Right now, simple things like splashing, feeling the warm water, and just being with you reinforces connections between brain cells!

Many babies enjoy a gentle massage after a bath. Make sure your baby is kept warm. Many oils and powders are not good for your baby's skin. Ask your doctor before using them. Talk or sing as both of you learn to enjoy this special time together.

Health

Make sure the room is warm enough for baths. Put your elbow in the water. It should be warm but not actually hot. Don't poke anything in your baby's ears, and take care to keep soap out of her eyes and mouth. Don't add bubble bath to the water.

Never leave your baby unattended in or near water, even if it's very shallow. Not even for one minute!

My Thoughts . . . Date

_____

_____

_____

_____

_____

_____

_____

_____

_____

_____

_____

_____

Caring, loving, and playing is important for your baby's brain development. Constantly ignoring her cries or regularly showing anger, stress, and tension can affect your baby's brain development in a negative way.

Week 5

When your baby is lying in his crib, hold a brightly colored object about 8 to 10 inches above his head. A rattle that makes a little noise will help get his attention. Slowly move the object back and forth as your baby watches it. This is called eye tracking. Stop when he's tired or not interested.

Your baby can focus his eyes on close objects for about one minute. Bold and bright colors are easiest to see. He can't see pastel and light colors very well yet.

You can attach a piece of poster board or other heavy paper to the side of your baby's crib that's against the wall. Paint simple, large, bold-colored patterns on it. A baby likes circles and curved lines better than straight ones. Change these often—babies get bored, too.

As your baby's eyesight gets stronger, move the crib around for different views.

Health

Don't give your baby cow's milk, water, juice, or any adult liquids. Solid foods and liquids usually begin at about 4 months of age (see Week 17). Until then, your baby is getting plenty of nourishment from breast milk or formula. Follow your doctor's advice.

Never leave your baby in a car unattended by an adult even if he's asleep. Always use a car seat.

My Thoughts . . . Date

_____

_____

_____

_____

_____

_____

_____

_____

_____

_____

_____

_____

Play with your baby only when he's alert and in a good mood. Playing is the way your baby builds his brain. If it's not enjoyable, or if it's boring, positive brain building doesn't happen.

25

Week 6

A comfortable rocking chair is relaxing for you and your baby. This can be a nice quiet time together for several years to come. (Perhaps you can find a good buy at a garage sale or secondhand store. You'll probably use it for many years.)

Cuddle and talk to your baby. Tell your baby stories about your life or dreams you have for her future. Play soft music or sing.

A calm environment is best for your baby. A baby is aware if people are angry, and this can be frightening. Try to keep your baby away from angry and loud arguments, even on the television. Don't play the television or music too loud. Comfort your baby when she's frightened.

Health

If you are breastfeeding and returning to work, call your hospital, a local LaLeche League or your local health department for a Women, Infants and Childrens (WIC) office near you. They can give you information about pumping and saving your milk. Don't heat milk in the microwave. It can get too hot for your baby.

Stimulating your baby's brain simply means that your baby is getting information to help build memory and skills. Information is coming from seeing, hearing, tasting, smelling, and touching.

My Thoughts . . . Date

_____

_____

_____

_____

_____

_____

_____

_____

_____

_____

Aside from being calming, rocking helps to develop certain parts of your baby's brain that are associated with balance and even language. It's very natural for mothers to do this. You will often find yourself rocking your baby when you are sitting or standing.

27

Week 7

Place your baby on his tummy on a blanket or thin mattress pad on the floor. Do this often when your baby is awake and alert. He needs to scoot around and eventually will learn how to crawl. This also helps him develop his neck and back muscles.

Some babies don't like to be on their tummies, but they need to build muscles so that they can lift their heavy heads. If your baby doesn't like being on his tummy, gently roll him over onto his back and in a short while, roll him over onto his tummy again. Dress him in clothes that are easy to move around in.

Get down on the floor and play with your baby. Sometimes he needs some company. A rattle or colorful toy will get his attention.

Safety

Don't leave a baby lying alone on a bed or couch. It's amazing how quickly they can move and fall off. Don't put your baby on his tummy on soft blankets or a soft mattress. Don't put pillows around him. This can make it hard or impossible for him to breathe. Always put your baby to sleep on his back.

Health

Schedule your baby's two-month doctor's visit and immunization. Write down any questions you have for the doctor. Immunizations protect your baby from life-threatening illnesses. He needs all of his immunizations on time to be protected. You'll need a record of these immunizations when he goes to childcare or school.

Have you noticed how intently your baby watches your eyes and mouth when you talk? Besides hearing words and sounds, this is helping him learn how to talk.

My Thoughts . . .   Date

_____

_____

_____

_____

_____

_____

_____

_____

_____

_____

The drive to learn is one of our most important instincts. Your baby is very eager to learn new skills, and you are his partner in this process. He smiles, cries, coos, and does other things to enlist your help. You'll begin to see the many signals that he's sending you as he begins this learning journey.

Week 8

It's really best to put your baby to bed without a bottle. Putting her to bed with a bottle can lead to problems with ear infections, choking, and baby bottle tooth decay. There are a number of ways you can put your baby to bed without a bottle.

- Feed and change her before bedtime.
- Sing or play music.
- Rub or pat her back.
- Hold or rock her to sleep.
- Pacifiers are often used, just don't use them all of the time, and don't dip them in honey or anything sweet.
- Your baby's thumb sucking is a natural way to calm herself.
- When she's a little older, she will probably have a favorite blanket or teddy bear that must go to bed with her.

Feeding

Make feeding a special time. Even if your life is busy, always hold your baby during feedings. Maintain eye contact and talk softly.

Health

Don't give your baby aspirin or other medicine without talking to the doctor first. Don't give your baby honey before two years of age. The germs in honey may cause illness or even death.

Babies suck on their thumbs for pleasure and security. It's one way they learn how to calm themselves.

My Thoughts . . .   Date

_____

_____

_____

_____

_____

_____

_____

_____

_____

_____

_____

_____

Try not to leave your baby lying in the crib or carrier
when she's awake and alert. This time is precious and it's
a time when important brain development takes place.
Simple activities like talking, smiling, and
cooing will influence your
baby's future success.

Week 9

When your baby makes cooing and other sounds, imitate and talk back to him. Wait for a minute to see if he has something to say. Act like you're talking to your best friend. To respond doesn't always mean talking. Smiling and body movements are also ways that he communicates with you. Your baby watches your face. Smile as you look in his eyes.

Babies do sense how you feel. If you're angry, find ways of cooling off before you pick up your baby. Make him feel loved in the way you touch him and talk to him.

Health

We all get angry and frustrated at times. When you're angry, don't take it out on your baby. Put your baby in a safe place. Call a friend, eat a snack, or take your baby for a walk. If you're almost always angry, talk to your doctor or other health professional. It's okay to ask for help.

Isn't it amazing that a baby knows what a smile means? He knows what a frown means too.

My Thoughts . . .   Date

_____

_____

_____

_____

_____

_____

_____

_____

_____

_____

_____

As your baby smiles and coos and you smile and coo back, you are "tuning in" and sharing feelings. Your baby is developing the capacity for joy and pleasure. When he cries and you pick him up and quietly tell him it's okay, he's learning that you understand him and that he can trust you to take care of him. This type of sharing has a very positive impact on your baby's life.

Week 10

Babies love different kinds of tunes, and it's good for their learning and brain development. Slow dance with your baby. Hold her head and neck securely because she can still be kind of wobbly. While dancing, spin slowly in a circle for about a minute and then stop. Count to ten. Circle the other way and stop again. This will help her balance later in life.

Look for some children's songs, and play them in the car or when you're rocking your baby. You can play patty-cake or other games to the music.

Health

Playing with your baby will bring pleasure and joy to your life and will relieve stress. As you dance around with your baby, you even get a little exercise.

Sing along with the music! It's great for reducing your stress, and it allows your baby to hear sounds and words.

My Thoughts . . .   Date

_____

_____

_____

_____

_____

_____

_____

_____

_____

_____

Play music softly. Loud music is not good for a baby's ears.
You might not listen to classical music often, but some
researchers think that this type of music helps to
develop the part of the brain that deals with
math and thinking. Try playing a little
classical music sometimes.

Week 11

Kiss, hug, and talk to your baby. Admire everything that he does—and tell him. The way that you talk to your baby now will have an impact on his ability to learn in the future and on his self-esteem.

In the early months, many of the important lessons a baby learns are with people. Warm and caring people will have the most positive influence on his future.

Picking up your baby when he cries lets him know that he is safe and that someone will take care of his needs. This will not spoil him. He is more likely to feel confident and good about himself as he grows up.

Child Care

Finding good child care can be difficult. Money is often a problem. But do your best to find someone that can give your baby individual attention in a place that's safe and clean. Ask often how your baby is doing, and stay involved.

Safety

Keep plastic bags away from your baby. He can chew and choke even on small pieces.

Even though your baby is getting heavier, carry him as often as possible. He doesn't get much time with you, and every minute counts.

My Thoughts . . .   Date

_____

_____

_____

_____

_____

_____

_____

_____

_____

_____

_____

_____

Even if you have good child care, your baby needs lots of attention from you. Sing and talk to him in the car. Play in the bath. Rock him and take a rest yourself. Bring him into the room you're working in, and talk to him.

Week 12

Prop your baby up a little with pillows. Have her grasp your fingers. Slowly and gently pull her up to a sitting position. Is she trying to help pull herself up? Tell her what a good job she's doing. Stop when she's tired.

How about a new fashion statement? Wear a special necklace for your baby to play with when you are holding her. Find some kind of strong cord, and string plastic measuring spoons or cups on it to make a necklace. Be creative. Babies love different textures, and it's good practice for them to use their hands and fingers.

Don't give your baby anything to play with that she can put around her neck, because she can choke herself with it.

Safety

Babies put everything in their mouths. Check everything carefully to be sure there are no buttons or anything else that could come off in her mouth.

Make sure there are no curtain pulls near the baby's crib (or anywhere else) that she can reach. It's alarming how babies can get wrapped up in them or get them around their necks.

What are some of the ways your baby has changed since bringing her home?

My Thoughts . . .   Date

_____

_____

_____

_____

_____

_____

_____

_____

_____

_____

_____

Don't leave your baby in a car seat or in a crib for long periods of
time. Even at this age, important mental and physical development
is taking place. Babies need to be able to move around
freely under supervision, and to be with people.
And NEVER leave baby in the car alone.

Week 13

Try to go to the grocery store when you're not in a big rush. This can be a great place for your baby's learning in the years to come. Talk about what you see and name different items as you go through the store. Don't be embarrassed if people stare at you. Most will be impressed by what a good parent you are.

Enjoy introducing your baby to this interesting place with all its sounds and smells. Think of it as a giant classroom where you are the teacher. Make this an adventure rather than a chore. Needless to say, this won't work if your baby's hungry or tired.

A light blanket in the colder areas of the store will keep your baby comfortable. It can also be used for peek-a-boo when waiting in a long line becomes boring.

Health

Cut your baby's fingernails when he's asleep. Don't have him wear mittens to keep him from scratching his face. He needs to move his hands and fingers freely. Dress your baby in layers so that you can keep him warm enough—not too hot and not too cold. Take off and put on as needed.

Your baby was born with about 100 billion brain cells. Brain building (stimulation) is about forming connections between the cells so they can efficiently communicate and work together.

My Thoughts . . .   Date

_____

_____

_____

_____

_____

_____

_____

_____

_____

_____

Whenever it's possible, let your baby touch and smell the things that you're buying. Get in the habit of counting how many apples or bananas you put in the cart. Count out loud as you tell him what you're doing. Are you buying a big box of cereal or a little can of tuna fish? He doesn't really understand now, but hearing different words is good for his learning.

Week 14

Propping up your baby in a sitting position will give her a whole new view on life. Roll a ball to her. She can't catch it yet, but watching (tracking) the ball is good for her developing eyesight.

Babies enjoy watching moving objects. Make a sock puppet for your hand using a bright-colored sock. Move it around slowly so that your baby watches it. Talk and make silly sounds. You can do this with your hands or fingers.

Your baby doesn't know things exist unless she can see them. Hide a toy under a pillow, pull it out and say, "Here's your teddy bear."

Put your face close, so your baby can touch you. Name the things she touches on your face (lips, nose, mouth, eyes and ears), and vice versa.

For right now, just give your baby one or two toys at a time. When she's bored, exchange them for one or two different toys. Keep in mind that toy means any object that's interesting to your baby. People often buy expensive toys and find that their baby has more fun with the wrapping and the box the toy came in.

Repeating words and actions helps to strengthen the new connections between brain cells. You'll find that you automatically repeat yourself and play peek-a-boo and other games over and over again.

My Thoughts . . .   Date

_____

_____

_____

_____

_____

_____

_____

_____

_____

_____

_____

_____

Babies like to repeat the skills they have just learned. This is an important part of their development. If your baby is bored with an activity, she will turn away or become fussy. This is a sure sign to stop.

43

Week 15

When your baby is on his tummy, he mostly sees the floor. Make it interesting for him. Take a large piece of poster board or cardboard—the bigger the better. Cut out bright pictures of large objects, and glue them on the board. Cover this with clear contact paper or laminate it. Let your baby play on this. (Later you can make smaller ones to put on tables and on the baby's high chair.)

Put a rattle right in front of him when he's on his tummy on the floor. He may become frustrated when he can't reach it, but let him try for a little while. This will encourage him to learn how to move and later to crawl.

Find a plastic bottle or jar with a large lid. Fill it halfway with water and put a rattle or other baby toy in it. Show your baby what it looks like when it rolls or when you shake it.

Put small toys in a round container, like an oat cereal box, and roll it around and shake it for different sounds.

Health

Make an appointment for your baby's four-month checkup and immunization. Make a list of questions to ask your doctor.

Get into the habit of reading to your baby each day. This will help his language development and, later, his reading abilities.

My Thoughts . . .   Date

_____

_____

_____

_____

_____

_____

_____

_____

_____

_____

_____

Your baby will probably first roll over by accident. This can be pretty surprising, and he might not know what to think of this major step. Let him know how happy you are, and what a big boy he is.

Week 16

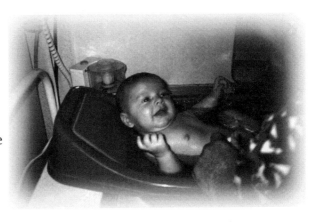

Bath time is a good playtime for your baby. Splashing water helps your baby learn how to move. She also is learning that she can make things happen. Show her how to splash with a wooden spoon or other toys. Have plastic containers for pouring water. Show her how to pour all the water out of a container and say, "All gone!"

Changing diapers can be made more fun too. Play peek-a-boo and tug of war with the diapers.

Instead of rushing to get your baby dressed, make this playtime.

Safety

Don't leave your baby alone in the bath for even one second.

Health

Diaper rash can be very painful. Change your baby often. Try to leave your baby's diapers off every once in a while.

Sometimes your baby may be tired and cranky and not in the mood to play.

My Thoughts . . .   Date

_____

_____

_____

_____

_____

_____

_____

_____

_____

_____

One of the things your baby is learning in these first years is what
she can expect from people. Do people listen to her?
Do they hug and love her? Does she get yelled
at if she tries to do something? If she gets yelled
at often, she'll be afraid to learn
and try new things.

47

Week 17

It's time now to feed your baby infant cereal. This will be a teaching experience for both of you. Be patient and have fun. Your baby actually needs to learn how to move his tongue and swallow food—a new skill that we simply take for granted. He may gag or spit up. Just take it slowly.

Your baby learns by imitating and watching you. Most parents find themselves eating baby cereal to show their baby how good it is.

Prepare the cereal with one tablespoon of breast milk or formula. Add enough cereal to make it a little runny. Feed it to your baby with a spoon and be patient. Talk to him about what you are doing in a calm manner.

Start with this small amount once a day. If there are no problems, increase the amounts.

Feeding

Don't put cereal in a bottle with formula or breast milk. Feed cereal to him slowly with a spoon. Putting cereal in a bottle can cause gas, diarrhea, or constipation. It can also cause choking.

Learning can be fun and it can be frustrating—for you and your baby. Babies often want to do activities their own way. Enjoy their creativity.

My Thoughts . . .   Date

_____

_____

_____

_____

_____

_____

_____

_____

_____

_____

_____

Is your baby watching your lips move as you talk? A baby
can tell when a mouth produces a particular vowel sound.
In effect, he is reading your lips. As he makes
different sounds he learns how to move
his mouth and tongue.

Week 18

Peek-a-boo is a game that your baby will love to play over and over again. Hide your face with your hands. Them remove them and say, "peek-a-boo." You can also cover your baby's face with her hands and say, "peek-a-boo."

You can also peek around corners or put a scarf over your face. Put the scarf over your baby's face with her hands and say, "peek-a-boo" when you pull it out. Hats work too.

Babies learn from watching their parents, even at this age. Set a good example—she's always watching you. Be polite to her and to others. Be careful about what you do and how you act when you're angry. It's easy to forget that she's there and watching.

Health

Always hold your baby when you are bottle feeding her. Babies left with a bottle propped up to feed them tend to have more ear infections. Constant ear infections can affect your baby's hearing. If you suspect any problems, contact your doctor and have your baby's hearing checked. Don't wait—it's never too early.

You and your baby are "communicating" in many different ways. Even most adult communication is nonverbal.

My Thoughts . . .   **Date**

_____

_____

_____

_____

_____

_____

_____

_____

_____

_____

Many games have been around for years. They are great for your baby's development. Ask older women about some of the things they did with their babies. Very simple games help your baby learn important skills. When your baby turns away, fusses, or cries, it's a good indication that she's ready to stop. Listen to her clues as to what she needs.

Week 19

Several times a week take 5 or 10 minutes and go around the house with your baby and name simple objects. Go slowly. Pick something up, and let him feel it (and smell it) as you name the object. You can name many of the same things each time. He won't get bored seeing the same things over and over again.

Wait a minute to see if he has something to say. Don't be in a rush. Babies like to turn things upside down and examine them from all sides. They like to feel different textures.

Point at objects so that he can begin to learn that pointing means to look at something. Play this game in the park or in the yard.

Health

Health care providers are usually pretty busy people, but your baby's health is very important. Call when you are concerned about something. Have a pencil and paper ready for instructions. Keep the phone number of your doctor, local pharmacy, and Poison Control handy.

Don't let your baby put plants or leaves in her mouth. They could be poisonous.

My Thoughts . . . **Date**

_____

_____

_____

_____

_____

_____

_____

_____

_____

_____

Babies love to do things over and over again. This is a necessary part of early learning. He will let you know when he's bored or tired. Looking away or fussing is one way that he lets you know. Forcing your baby to learn something when he's not in the mood will only be stressful for both of you.

Week 20

B e a cheerleader. Every time your baby does something, tell her how wonderful she is. In fact, as your child is growing up, this will always be important.

Babies are learning machines. Everything they do adds to their learning development. They want to learn and are constantly looking for opportunities. Slow down and enjoy this amazing time. Watch for what your baby is interested in, and give her time to explore it.

Your baby does understand when she has made you happy and proud of her. She wants to please you. When she does, she knows it's safe and okay for her to learn and explore.

It doesn't take a lot of money to provide a good learning environment.

Health

Sometimes mothers have problems with depression. If you are often sad, crying, or always tired and depressed, call your doctor or health care professional for help. If you don't take care of this, it can have long-lasting negative effects on your baby's development.

Act happy around your baby as often as possible.

My Thoughts . . .   Date

_____

_____

_____

_____

_____

_____

_____

_____

_____

_____

Don't use television as a babysitter. Hearing words on television doesn't help your baby learn how to talk. The bright colors and fast moving objects on TV may interest your baby, but there is a concern about how this may affect a baby's ability to pay attention in school at a later age.

Week 21

When handing your baby a rattle or other small toy, hold it far enough away from him to make him reach out for it. Have him reach high, low, and to both sides. Sometimes put things in his left hand and sometimes in the right hand. Make a game of this.

If he is interested in something that he's doing, let him have as much time with that activity as he wants. Often, he'll be adding to his understanding of something. Giving him the time to do what interests him is important to his learning development. Remember this as your baby gets older.

Health

There are a lot of opinions about when to feed your baby solid foods and what those solid foods might be. Use your best judgment about what is best for your baby. All babies are different and, like adults, all have different tastes.

Some new foods can now be given. Give just one new food a week, and see how he does with it. Start with vegetables. Try carrots, potatoes, or broccoli. If you give fruit first, he may become used to the sweet taste and refuse to eat vegetables later. Don't give your baby any citrus fruits (such as oranges and grapefruit) in his first year.

Feeding

Instead of canned baby food, you can easily cook your own. Cook vegetables (like a carrot) in a little water until it is very soft. Mash it with a fork (or put in a blender), and mix until it looks like mashed potatoes. Don't add salt or sugar.

Don't use microwave ovens for heating milk or food for your baby. The heat can be uneven and burn your baby.

My Thoughts . . . Date

_____

_____

_____

_____

_____

_____

_____

_____

_____

_____

_____

Making your baby reach helps with coordination, and reaching across the body also helps brain development. He needs to learn how to use both hands. He was born either right-handed or left-handed, so this kind of play will not change that.

Week 22

Hold your baby up to a mirror and show her what she looks like. Name parts of her face and body. Have her touch her own nose and yours too. Name each part as you touch it. Put a child-safe mirror on the side of the baby's crib so that she can see herself. Who is this interesting person?

Babies love being with others, and it helps them to learn new things. Bring your baby into the same room with you when she's not sleeping. Some babies just want to know that you're close by in case they need you.

Dad is an important part of a baby's life. Babies do better later in life when Dad is involved. Try to have uncles and granddads play with baby too.

Feeding

Give your baby a baby cup or sipper cup to play with. Let her chew on it and imitate you drinking from a cup. Let her get used to handling it for a week or two, then put a small amount of breast milk or formula in it.

Think "out loud" when you are around your baby. The more words she hears, the better.

My Thoughts . . . Date

_____

_____

_____

_____

_____

_____

_____

_____

_____

_____

_____

_____

Babies need to be with people in order to get the experiences necessary to grow healthy brains. Overworked parents often don't have lots of time to spend with their baby, but any time spent will be worthwhile. Look for opportunities to spend time with your baby.

Week 23

Encourage crawling by putting your baby on the floor as much as possible. Put one or two toys just out of reach.

Toys that can be pushed along the floor encourage your baby to crawl. As babies often make up their own toys, you may find your baby pushing a box or other container along the floor.

When your baby does crawl, make toys easy to get to. Open shelves are easy to get to but will look messy. Your baby's learning is more important than keeping things neat.

Safety

Get down on the floor and look around for things that could hurt your baby. Look around often for small objects that your baby will put in his mouth. Take anything off tables that you don't want him to have or that could fall on him. Always keep plastic bags away from your baby. House plants can be poisonous.

Feeding

Put a little formula or breast milk into your baby's cup, and show him how to drink from it. Give him milk in the cup before you give him juice. You want him to learn to enjoy milk from a cup so that he doesn't always want sweet drinks.

Lay down on the floor with your baby and relax a bit.

My Thoughts . . .   Date

_____

_____

_____

_____

_____

_____

_____

_____

_____

Safety means more than just physical safety. Your baby needs to feel that he's safe emotionally. This means that you're nearby in case he needs you and that he won't be unjustly punished or yelled at for experimenting. Remember that one of the primary ways he's learning is by touching things. Make areas in your home a "baby friendly" environment.

Week 24

I t's likely that many people will care about your baby and add to her development and happiness. Right now, your baby can't get too much attention from people who are loving. Hopefully most of these people will be in her life for a long time.

As difficult as it can be to find good child care, try your best to find someone who will be with your child on a more or less permanent basis. It's upsetting to babies when caretakers are changed often, and it can harm their long-term development.

Make a "feel good" blanket. Collect different kinds of fabric and things like fake fur. Use things that feel different. Cut them up in large pieces, and sew them onto a small blanket or towel. (Silk, cotton, felt, and old fuzzy blankets will all work.)

Don't use buttons or anything that might come off. Use washable fabrics, and don't worry if this blanket looks kind of funny.

Health

When your baby is six months old, her brain will weigh twice as much as it did when she was born. She needs different experiences so that she can build her memory and learn how to figure things out. She needs healthy food for her growing body and her growing brain.

Play is food for the brain.

My Thoughts . . . Date

_____

_____

_____

_____

_____

_____

_____

_____

_____

_____

Your baby's brain is gathering information through all of her senses. Sight, smell, hearing, seeing, and touch, all provide "food" for the rapidly growing brain. Creating interesting and enjoyable experiences is not complicated. It's called Play!

Week 25

Babies seem to like things that are new to them. They find them more interesting. Don't worry, you can bring out something that your baby hasn't seen for a week or two and it will seem "new" to him.

Toys are becoming more interesting now, but your baby will often like you or Dad to be part of the play. He thinks it's very funny when you stack small boxes or blocks and then knock them down. He'll be able to knock things down, but it will be harder to learn how to stack them.

Babies like things that make noises. Put smaller toys into large plastic jars (one that have large lids) and show him how to shake or roll them. Take the lid off, and let the toys fall to the ground. You can also use paper bags.

Babies enjoy playing with household objects just as much as store-bought toys. The kitchen is one of the best places for great toys. Wooden spoons, plastic measuring cups, and pans will interest your baby.

Wash and save all sizes and kinds of empty containers. Save small boxes.

Save old hats, purses, and cloth bags. You will need to cut off any long handles that might get wrapped around your baby's neck. You'll be surprised at how many things become safety hazards around your curious baby.

Babies often want to do activities their own way. Enjoy their creativity.

My Thoughts . . .   Date

_____

_____

_____

_____

_____

_____

_____

_____

_____

_____

_____

Your baby will have his own way of playing with containers. This is part of learning how to think and solve problems. He might decide that a bowl makes a great hat. Cans can be rolled or stacked. Enjoy your baby's inventions.

Week 26

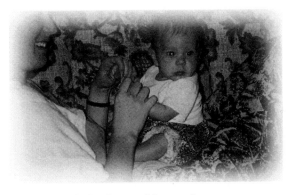

Your baby is communicating with you in many ways. It's important for her to realize that you're getting her message. Smiling, reaching for something, and crying are all attempts to get a message across.

When your baby is "talking," listen and answer her just as if she has told you the most important thing in the world. Sometimes, make the same sounds she has made, and watch her reactions.

If she shows you that she wants something out of reach, hand it to her and name the object. Some babies show that they want something by looking at it. Always try to respond. You'll soon find that you've become a pretty good mind reader.

If she wants something that she can't have, tell her she can't have that, but give her something else that she can have, or give her a choice of two things that she may play with.

Watch to see if your baby is looking at something that you're looking at. Name the object. Point at different things as you talk about them.

Health

Your baby's eyesight is pretty well developed by now, but there are some things that could indicate a problem. Talk to your doctor if your baby's eyes are crossed, bulge, or are red and tearing. Do your baby's eyes look normal? Doctors are able to check eyesight at a very early age.

You won't spoil your baby with too much attention.

My Thoughts . . .   Date

_____

_____

_____

_____

_____

_____

_____

_____

_____

_____

_____

_____

Babies are very sensitive to your signals and emotions. How fast you respond to her cries of distress affects her sense of well being. She'll feel more confident in exploring her world when she knows you are close by. Some babies are more confident than others. Be sensitive to your baby's needs.

Week 27

When your baby is able to sit upright, place him in a high chair. The high chair is a place to eat and a good place for playing when you're in the kitchen. Strap him in safely. Stay nearby.

Put an old plastic tablecloth under the high chair to catch spills. Don't leave your baby alone in his high chair.

Put a small amount of round oat cereal on the table (not sugar coated), and let him try to pick it up. He may begin by using his whole hand, but after some practice, he'll begin using his fingers.

Give him a spoon and a small bowl of water to play with. Show him how you use a spoon. He probably has other ideas, but this is a beginning.

Don't let him stuff his mouth with food. He can choke. Give your baby just a little bit of food at a time.

Feeding

Soft cooked pinto beans are good for your baby, and he can try to pick them up by himself.

Health

Most babies double their birth weight when they reach about six months of age.

It's time for your baby's six-month doctor's appointment and immunization. Write down any questions for the doctor.

My Thoughts . . .

Date

_____

_____

_____

_____

_____

_____

_____

_____

_____

_____

_____

_____

Hand skills are important to practice. Picking up small objects can be a pretty hard thing to learn how to do. When your baby has learned how to pick up small things, you have to watch closely. As you have already learned, everything goes into the mouth.

Week 28

Find a nice medium-sized box (a shoe box works) with a lid. Bring out a couple of your baby's favorite small toys. On the lid of the box, cut holes big enough that the toys will fit through. This will be a "hiding place."

Take one of the toys and show her how it fits into the hole. Where is it? Look around and then take off the lid. Surprise! There it is!

Your baby will learn how to put the toys in the holes, and she'll learn that something exists even if she can't see it.

Your baby's brain is rapidly growing and making connections. The 100 billion brain cells have one trillion supporting cells. The nerve cells make 1,000 trillion synaptic contact points (connections) with each other. This number is far greater than all the stars and all the planets in the Milky Way.

Some of the connections that are not used will be pruned away, just like weeding a garden. This is normal. The connections that are left are the ones that are used often.

This information isn't for you to remember, it's to let you know what a huge job your baby has. And, hugs and play mostly accomplish it.

Health

Clean or brush your baby's teeth with a small tooth brush daily. Don't use toothpaste. Your baby cannot spit it out.

Baby bottle tooth decay can be a problem if you put your baby to bed with a bottle or if she carries around a bottle often during the day. Tooth decay is painful. If it does develop, it can cause chewing problems and even speech problems. Take your baby to the dentist right away if you notice problems.

Love is smiling even when you're tired.

My Thoughts . . . Date

_____

_____

_____

_____

_____

_____

_____

_____

_____

_____

It takes your baby a little while to learn what you are showing her, so don't rush. Along the way, both of you will be learning new things. Also, you might think about how you can slow down your schedule and have more time to enjoy your baby. Literally, stop and smell the roses.

Week 29

ake books for your baby using large pictures from magazines or pictures of real people. Cut out large, simple, real looking objects that your baby is familiar with (balls, dogs, cups, food—very simple objects).

Put these into a photo album or paste them on thick paper. If you are making your own album, put two or three holes in the side and tie with ribbon. Cover with clear contact paper.

Point to the objects, and make up stories about them. Does your baby have anything to say? Let him help you if he wants to. You can hold him or put the book on a table so that he can help turn the pages. If he shows interest in something, let him take his time.

Memory is important to all of us, and your baby is just beginning to develop his. Not only does he need to develop memory, he also needs to learn how to use his memory. We don't remember our early years because we didn't know how to remember. Complicated, isn't it?

Feeding

You can begin to offer your baby two or three ounces of water or diluted juice in his baby cup. Mix juice with half water. Apple juice or white grape juice is often recommended. Don't put juice in a bottle. This can be bad for his teeth. Remember, no citrus juice for the first year. Some babies are allergic to oranges, grapefruit, and strawberries.

You can make up stories and use your imagination when you read to your baby.

My Thoughts . . .   Date

_____

_____

_____

_____

_____

_____

_____

_____

_____

_____

_____

As with any activity, reading should be enjoyable. Early reading is not about learning how to read, but about spending special time together and hearing different words. Stop when your baby is tired or bored.

Week 30

Teach your baby how to dance. Hold her with your hands under her arms. Help her move in time with the music. She'll soon be making up her own dances. This helps balance and coordination and builds strong legs.

Sing along as you dance with your baby. This is another opportunity for language development.

Let your baby go barefoot in the house (or just wear a pair of socks).

Play different kinds of music, but not too loud. While you have the music on, give her a wooden spoon and a pan or box to pound on.

You might soon notice your baby pointing at things, but she doesn't know what this means yet. She's just practicing—like babbling before she actually talks.

Even though your baby is developing trillions of connections in her brain, there's no need to continually bombard her with activities. Relax a bit. She has a strong drive to learn and will keep you on track.

Health

Baby walkers are not recommended for several reasons. They are unsafe and do not help children learn to walk. Your baby needs to learn balance, and only learning how to walk the old-fashioned way—by trial and error—does this. Giver her lots of opportunity to move around in a safe environment.

Babies begin walking at many different ages. Let her develop at her own pace.

My Thoughts . . . Date

_____

_____

_____

_____

_____

_____

_____

_____

_____

_____

Every time you give your baby a hug and tell her what a good job she did, she gains confidence. It can be hard to decide when to help your baby do something and when to let her keep trying. Don't be too quick to step in. But your baby also needs to be successful. Watch and just do the best job you can. If she falls when trying to stand up, wait a minute and see if she recovers by herself.

Week 31

A baby learning how to feed himself can be fun and very messy. Give your baby a small spoon. Very likely, he will often decide his hands are much better. Be patient and just hand him the spoon now and then.

He learns from watching you, so have your own spoon ready! Yummy.

Babies like to feed themselves. Crackers and dry cereals are easy for your baby. Just be careful that he doesn't stuff his mouth and choke. Give him a little at a time. Other foods he might like are unsalted soda crackers, soft tortillas, pieces of cheese, and banana.

Find an old plastic tablecloth for under the highchair. This can be used when your baby is playing in the highchair and it is easier to clean up.

Feeding

Your baby needs iron-rich foods like beans and pureed meats. He can have trouble digesting or be allergic to certain foods. Just give him one new food at a time and wait four or five days before trying a new food. Don't add salt, sugar or honey.

Take pictures! They'll be fun to see years from now.

My Thoughts . . .   Date

_____

_____

_____

_____

_____

_____

_____

_____

_____

_____

Many of the best learning activities are messy. Finger painting, splashing water all over the place, playing in the dirt, and many others require time that you don't really have to clean up. It really is worth making the time.

Week 32

Pointing is a big step in your baby's ability to communicate with you. She can show you what she wants and what looks interesting to her. When she sees that you understand her communication, it encourages her to communicate even more.

Pay attention to what she is pointing at. Talk about it, and if it is something that she can have, give it to her.

Give your baby choices by pointing. Do you want this ball or this truck? Watch for clues from her about what she wants.

If she wants something that she can't have, offer her something that she can have. "No, you can't have the cookie, but you can have a piece of banana."

Or, "No, you can't have that, but let's go see Daddy".

Try not to make things a constant power struggle. Give a little thought to your decisions. When she gets what she wants, it gives her confidence. On the other hand, she will need to learn that she won't always get what she wants. This lesson will begin in later years. Right now she doesn't have the ability to think things out.

Waving bye-bye and pointing to things teaches your baby "sign language." This encourages language development.

My Thoughts . . .   Date

_____

_____

_____

_____

_____

_____

_____

_____

_____

_____

Offering another object or activity in place of something you don't want your baby to have (or to do) is a useful parenting tool in the upcoming years. It gives her some choice and power, but you're still the boss. This is called "redirecting" by child care providers and professionals. You redirect your child's attention. (It doesn't always work, but give it a try!)

Week 33

Make an apron out of felt. Or buy an apron and sew on pieces of felt where you want the Velcro to stick. It doesn't have to be fancy. Put in a pocket or two. Attach Velcro tabs in various places. Attach Velcro to a number of stuffed animals, balls, plastic measuring spoons, and other small toys.

You become a walking toy box. If you have company or are on the phone, or just want to sit and relax, you have toys right there for your baby to play with.

When you're in the car, use a short piece of string or ribbon (about six inches long) to tie one or two toys to the crossbar on the car seat. When your baby throws them, they are just a short distance away. You can use this for the stroller too.

Don't use any long pieces of string or ribbon. Anything your baby can get around his neck can be dangerous.

Health

Prevent lead poisoning. Keep your baby away from chipped paint. (This includes the paint on his crib.) It may contain lead. If he chews or swallows this, it can make him sick and harm his development. If you live in an older home that might have lead paint on the walls, keep floors and furniture well dusted with a damp cloth or mop. Handmade or imported pottery or dishes can contain lead. Do not use with food or drinks.

Dirt outside of the house can contain lead from peeling paint or car exhaust. Keep your baby clean and wash hands and toys.

At your baby's one year check-up, (or if you think there may be a problem), ask for a blood test to be run. This is the only way you will know if your baby has too much lead in his system.

Some house keys contain dangerous amounts of lead. There's no way to tell if they do or don't, so keep these away from your baby.

My Thoughts . . . Date

Babies have lots of curiosity. The more you
encourage this curiosity, the more they
will learn and build a strong foundation
for later development and learning.

Week 34

Find a special place in the kitchen that your baby can use for "her things." If you don't have cupboard space, an old laundry basket or box will do. Babies love to put things in and take things out.

She can play while you fix meals. Stop your work occasionally, and enjoy her play and praise her work.

Rather than telling her how to play with something, let her have as much freedom as possible so that she can try new and different things. She does need you to step in every once in a while and show her new things that she might try.

Remember, there is no "right way" to use a measuring spoon or stack small boxes. This is creativity at its best.

Safety

As fun as the kitchen can be, it can also be dangerous for your baby. Go through the lower cupboards and drawers, and remove anything that could hurt her. Put these things up high or in a safe place. Look under the sink and remove bug sprays and other chemicals. Keep soap out of reach. Put a childproof lock on this door. Don't let your baby play with empty dish soap containers.

Touching is an important method your baby uses to get information into her brain.

My Thoughts . . .   Date

_____

_____

_____

_____

_____

_____

_____

_____

_____

_____

When you talk about what you're doing or what you see, you are
adding new sounds and words to your baby's developing
language abilities. Using a lot of new words helps
develop a larger capacity for vocabulary. You
don't need to get out your dictionary.
Reading and talking is just fine.

Week 35

When your baby talks to you, it's called "babbling." He's experimenting with his mouth, tongue, and jaw. He thinks this is fun, and it's helping him learn how to talk. Make these sounds back to him.

Talking is a major skill that your baby will begin to learn in his first year. Even though it will be a long time before he actually says words, his brain has been hard at work laying the foundation for words and understanding.

You'll probably notice that you're not talking "baby talk" as much (except when you are imitating your baby's sounds). Parents have a natural instinct about how to talk to their babies.

Talk to your baby in the same way you talk to your best friends. Be pleasant and let your baby take his turn in the conversation. Once in a while, say, "I'm going to feed you now," rather than "Mommy is going to feed you now." It can be hard for a baby to learn the difference between you, him, her, and me. Use these words when you talk.

Health

All infants "babble" even if they have hearing problems. If he stops babbling, it can be a sign that he can't hear himself. Have his hearing checked. It's important to know if he has a hearing problem. It's often far easier to correct problems if they are found at an early age.

Safety

Keep medicines and vitamin pills away from your baby. Don't keep medicine in your purse. When giving your baby medicine, do not call it candy.

You may want to look for a book on baby sign language. It will be fun for both you and your baby.

My Thoughts . . .   **Date**

_____

_____

_____

_____

_____

_____

_____

_____

_____

_____

Your baby's brain was designed to learn how to talk. He's very eager to communicate with you. He began to learn sound patterns in the very first days after birth. Now he's beginning to distinguish individual words. (If you listen to others, you can hear that a sentence often sounds like just one word.) He's already learned how to take his turn in conversation, just as adults do.

Week 36

Make a texture book just for your baby. Collect small items around the house that feel different and are different sizes. For instance, you may find pieces of fabrics that are different sizes and different colors. Find leaves that are different sizes, shapes, and colors. (Don't let your baby put leaves in her mouth—they could be poisonous.)

Use different colors and different textures of paper and fabric. Make it fun and interesting. Use heavy paper so that your baby can read and touch this book. Tell stories as you look through the book. Point and let her touch. Touching is what this book is made for.

Since this book may have things that your baby could choke on, put it away when you're not with her. Make it a special reward to play with it.

Health

It's time for your baby's nine-month check-up and immunization. Make a list of any questions for the doctor.

Feeding

When buying baby foods, buy single-ingredient foods, such as strained chicken or beef. You get more protein for your money. Give your baby one or two tablespoons a day. Don't give her bacon, bologna, hot dogs, peanut butter, and other things with a lot of salt and sugar. Don't give her sweet fruit drinks.

It's easy to get in the habit of saying, "Don't touch that" without even thinking. Your baby learns by touching, so let her touch things that are safe.

My Thoughts . . .   **Date**

_____

_____

_____

_____

_____

_____

_____

_____

_____

_____

When your child is exposed to a variety of experiences early in life, she will more easily tap into her natural abilities and talents. Again, there is no need to run yourself ragged. But as your child grows and develops, think of enjoyable things to do and places to see.

Week 37

Take an empty paper bag and put things in it for your baby to feel. Start with just one item. Hide it in the bag, and let him put his hand in to feel what it is. Let him pull it out and see what it is.

During a quiet time, ask your baby what he hears. Does he hear someone coming to the door? A dog barking? Shhhh...listen. Do this often to help your baby become a better listener.

Play "What is that?" This can be in the house, car, or yard. Point to something and say, "What is that?" "Is that a kitty?"

Even though your baby can't talk yet, he'll enjoy this silly game for several years. It's great for language and memory development.

Continue both activities as your baby gets older.

Not all activities will appeal to your baby.

Safety

Your baby wants to put everything in his mouth to learn about it. As you know, this can sometimes be very dangerous. Babies can get even fairly large objects stuck in their throats.

One way to measure objects is to take an empty toilet paper roll and see if the object can fit through the middle of it. If it can, it's too small to let your baby play with it. Make sure small parts cannot break away from larger objects.

Look for things that your baby can look at, touch, hear, and smell.

My Thoughts . . .   **Date**

_____

_____

_____

_____

_____

_____

_____

_____

_____

_____

_____

Make time for fun. Play is food for your baby's brain and it's good for you, too. Not having enough time is one of the biggest obstacles for parents. There's a term for this — Time Poverty. You don't need a lot of money to raise a bright child, but you do need a lot of time.

Week 38

Empty paper towel, toilet paper, and cardboard gift-wrap rolls can be used in different ways. Save them. Your baby will play with them as they are, but you can also make things. Find a box with a lid. Cut two round holes in the lid that toilet paper tubes will fit into. You can decorate the box with bright colors.

Show her how the tubes fit into the holes. If she wants to do other things, let her. Show her again later how the tubes can fit in the holes. Let her find her own way of doing this and playing with this box. Babies can get very involved when trying new things.

Your baby may not be ready or interested in some of these activities yet. Some can be used for several years. Mark those that you want to remember so you can quickly go back and find them.

Safety

Keep syrup of ipecac on hand in case of a poison emergency. Don't use it unless told to do so by the Poison Control Center or your doctor. Check to see if you have emergency numbers handy.

Don't be disappointed if your baby's not ready for a suggested activity.

My Thoughts . . . Date

_____

_____

_____

_____

_____

_____

_____

_____

_____

_____

_____

_____

Many babies are shy or afraid of strangers. Don't force her to go to someone, just take it slowly. And don't be embarrassed if she's suddenly afraid of a good friend. She needs to know that you're there.

Week 39

Some babies crawl, some scoot, and some roll. All of these are fine. Your baby has his own timetable. All babies have a big desire to get someplace. This is a built-in desire that will lead to walking.

Babies are able to learn a lot more when they can explore their small world. Their world gets bigger as they go from hardly moving to crawling and then to walking. Every step leads to more things to hear, touch, taste, see, and smell.

A small mark on the floor might be very interesting to your baby as he returns again and again to try to pick it up. Your baby is really quite good at managing much of his learning development. He is very interested in figuring things out. Let him take his time.

Make areas safe and be interested in what your baby is doing. Babies often enjoy being funny and getting your attention. They like knowing that people pay attention to what they are doing. This gives them confidence, and they know they are important.

Safety

Balloons are a choking hazard for babies. They should never be given to babies or small children.

Your baby might be very involved with something one minute, and then the next minute he might cry to be picked up.

My Thoughts . . . Date

_____

_____

_____

_____

_____

_____

_____

_____

_____

Brain cells are somewhat like trees with branches sprouting from them. Cells can have 20,000 branches that reach out to connect to other branches. With even simple experiences, your baby is developing a rich network of branches. He's quickly developing a strong foundation for learning and thinking.

93

Week 40

Back to the grocery store activities! Hand small unbreakable things to your baby so that she can put them in the basket for you. Talk to her about what you give her. Ask her if she likes it. She might want to keep it for awhile. Let her make these decisions. Of course, the problem with this is that she will want to open it.

Does she think you should get some carrots? Potatoes? Crackers? Where are you going next? Let's get some bread. Point in the direction that you will be going to next.

Show her a big box and a small box of cereal. Which will you get? Do we get the big one or the small one?

As she gets older, she can participate more and more. Put things on the scale and weigh them. How much does a melon weigh? What about an apple?

When you get home, let your baby help to put things away. Where does the milk go?

Your baby doesn't understand all of this, but she's hearing new words and you are getting into the natural habit of teaching math, language, and reading.

Feeding

Your baby can eat some of the foods you fix for the family now. Don't give her nuts, seeds, raw carrots, or other small hard foods (such as popcorn) that she could choke on. Don't force your baby to eat anything she doesn't want. First of all, you'll lose. Second, your baby's likes and dislikes will change very fast.

How many times have you said, "I have to do that before I understand it."? Babies have to do things, too, not just watch.

My Thoughts . . .   Date

Big or small is one of your baby's first math lessons. So is "all
gone." Talk about sizes and shapes and colors. Ask her
questions to get her involved. Cut her food into two
or three pieces and count them. Fill her cup
half full. Use words like half or full.
Don't make this a big "lesson."

Week 41

Put your baby in his high chair for finger painting. Mix a few crumbs with yogurt or Jell-O. Pudding will also work. Look in the refrigerator for some interesting "stuff" (like cooked rice) that won't hurt him if he eats it. (He will!) Put an old plastic tablecloth on the floor, and stay nearby.

This can keep your baby busy while you're cooking dinner or just relaxing. Admire his creativity. You can also give him things like a wooden spoon, plastic measuring cups, and non-breakable bowls. Smearing is messy, but great for developing small muscles and for your baby to learn how to control and use his fingers.

Safety

Don't leave your baby alone in the high chair, and be sure to strap him in.

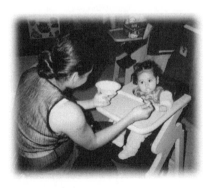

Feeding

Gradually give more foods. Tasty mashed potatoes are healthy and easy to fix. Peel and boil a carrot and a potato. Cook until they are soft, and then mash them together. Add a little breast milk or formula. (Don't add salt or butter.) Don't let your baby have too much juice or milk. He needs to eat solid foods for good health.

Take pictures of some of your baby's "artwork" and start a photo album.

My Thoughts . . .   **Date**

Your baby inherits certain genes from the family but how these genes develop is very much influenced by the environment and things that he experiences.

Week 42

Building blocks for building brains. Find small pieces of hard wood and sand them to make blocks. Use different sizes and shapes. (Don't have any sharp pieces that might hurt her if she falls on them.)

She will be playing with blocks for a long time, so you're not wasting your time by making these.

You can also make blocks by filling small boxes with cornmeal and covering them with contact paper to seal well. Or, just use empty boxes of different sizes and shapes.

Get into the habit of counting things. Count blocks as you hand them to your baby or stack them. Count the stairs as you walk up them. Count out pieces of cereal. This is much different than memorizing meaningless numbers on a sheet of paper. Don't drill—just count.

Your baby won't learn how to count yet, but she will begin to understand what numbers mean. You'll see just how much she understands numbers when she wants three cookies instead of two!

Safety

As your baby begins to get around more and more, there are increased opportunities for injury. Pick up information on safety tips, and keep your eyes open and stay alert.

Old fashioned toys like building blocks are great for building brains.

My Thoughts . . .   Date

_____

_____

_____

_____

_____

_____

_____

_____

_____

_____

Memorizing letters or numbers from flash cards at this age has no meaning for your baby. It's somewhat like riding a bicycle before you can walk. Forced learning too early can create pressure and be more of a negative influence than a positive one. Remember the words "play" and "fun."

Week 43

This game will be fun for several years. Face your baby and take one of his hands. Hold out his palm and face it up to the ceiling. Take his other hand and wrap his fingers up like he's pointing at something. Hold both hands and as you sing, poke his finger into his palm to the rhythm of the music.

You can make up silly songs like "Boom, boom, boom, the cow jumped over the moon. Boom, boom, boom, the cat ran away with the spoon." Change hands once in awhile.

At this age, your baby can understand quite a few words even if he can't speak. When he says something, let him use his own words. If he says ba-ba for blanket, hand him the blanket and say, "Here's your blanket." If he points to something, hand it to him and say, "Here's your ball."

Have you noticed you just can't think when you're stressed? It's the same thing for your baby. A lot of stress is not good for the brain.

My Thoughts . . . Date

_____

_____

_____

_____

_____

_____

_____

_____

_____

_____

_____

It's not necessary to make your baby say the "right" word. Simply repeat what he has said correctly. He'll get the idea and correct himself when he's ready. Right now, it's more important that you encourage his talking by responding to his message.

Week 44

Fill a plastic dishpan or large bowl with clean sand, cornmeal, or rice. Get out a wooden spoon, a funnel, plastic cups, or other kitchen items. Show your baby how to put sand in the cup with a spoon or how to pour sand through the funnel.

Babies will often play by themselves with these household toys for a long time. Ask her what she is doing sometimes. Ask her if she can put sand in the big cup or the yellow spoon. Talking about the objects will teach her about colors, bigger and smaller, all gone, and fill it up. These concepts will help her in her math classes years from now.

You can also use water with all of the above objects. In the summer, filling a small plastic pool with a couple of inches of water is lots of fun.

Safety

Babies can drown in as little as two inches of water. Never leave your baby alone for one second in the bath or wading pool.

Health

Use sunscreen when you take your baby outside. Better yet, keep her in the shade as much as possible.

Babies don't necessarily make things or say things the "right way." Don't make your baby "wrong" or "stupid." It's okay to make mistakes.

My Thoughts . . . Date

_____

_____

_____

_____

_____

_____

_____

_____

_____

Computers for infants? Many researchers feel that time spent on this activity would be better spent in old-fashioned play and being with people. One thing to consider is eyesight. Another thing is repetitive hand and wrist movement that might damage growth.

Week 45

Get a flashlight and shine it against the wall in a dark room. Play some slow music and move the light with the music. Let your baby try it. Go around the room looking at different things. Where's the lamp? Where's the door?

Go outside and look at things with the flashlight at night.

Some babies are ready to use crayons at this age. Get very large non-toxic ones. Don't make your baby hold them the right way. Let him hold them any way that he wants to. His hands and fingers are not ready yet to hold them like you do.

Feeding

Fix healthy meals for the whole family. Here's an easy recipe for nutritious soup.

Meatball Soup

Ingredients:

1 can chicken broth	3 cups water
1 carrot, diced	1 stalk celery, diced
1 egg	½ cup crushed crackers
1 lb. ground round	1 zucchini, sliced

Directions:

Add chicken broth to water and bring to a boil. Add carrot and celery to mixture. Cook 10 minutes. While it is cooking, make the meatballs.

Mix raw egg and crushed crackers with ground round. Roll into small balls (like Ping-Pong balls) and add to the soup.

Cook for about 20 more minutes. Add sliced zucchini to the soup and cook for another 15 minutes. For the baby, mash up mostly vegetables and meatballs with a little broth.

Safety

Don't let your baby have the flashlight when you're not there. The batteries could be harmful if they leak.

Your busy baby is working hard to grow and develop his brain.

My Thoughts . . .   Date

_____

_____

_____

_____

_____

_____

_____

_____

_____

_____

_____

You are a partner in your baby's exploration of the world. Enjoying and encouraging his curiosity lays the foundation for his love of learning throughout life.

Week 46

Give your baby old purses, backpacks, or bags to keep special things in. Cut off any long straps. At first you can give her things to put in the bag. Soon, she'll have her own ideas about what to put into her bags.

Sit down with her on the floor and talk to her about what she has in her bags. Ask her questions about what she's going to put into her purse. Name each item as it goes in. Ask her to find something from her treasures. Ask silly questions. Does the dog fit into her purse? Does the chair? Being silly makes it fun and a valuable thinking lesson.

If you don't want to give your baby boy a purse, how about a plastic lunch box, or some type of canvas carrying bag.

Safety

Keep your baby away from straps or cords that could wrap around her neck and choke her. Six or seven inches is considered a safe length.

Health

It's never too early to eat healthy foods. If you're going to be out for awhile, pack a picnic lunch or snack. Pack some cheese, crackers, and a banana. If you're able to do this often, get your baby her own little lunch box.

How creative are you at finding "toys" around the house?

My Thoughts . . .   Date

_____

_____

_____

_____

_____

_____

_____

_____

_____

Encourage imagination by getting out old hats, scarves, and shoes. These kinds of things are better for learning than expensive toys. Imagination leads to better thinking skills and problem solving.

Week 47

Get a large magnifying glass and take walks through the house, the yard, and the park. Let your baby take an active part in this as soon as he gets the idea. Point to different things to look at, and go over to that object. What does an ant look like?

Get excited about what your baby wants to look at. This is great learning for both of you. It's never too early for a science lesson.

You can collect items to paste on a large piece of paper while you're out on a walk. Keep them in a bag for later artwork activities. Or, you can save them to talk about and touch afterward.

Health

After eating, while your baby is still in his high chair, give him a small soft toothbrush to chew on. He's probably watched you brush your teeth and will try to imitate you. When he starts to brush his teeth in the bathroom, remember no toothpaste. Babies can't spit until they are about three years old.

Very young children who watch a lot of television seem to have lower grades in school. (Yes, this includes videos.)

My Thoughts . . .   Date

_____

_____

_____

_____

_____

_____

_____

_____

_____

_____

Make sure your baby understands that when you point at something, you want him to look at it. This is an important step in his communication development. Talk to your doctor if you don't think he understands this. Every baby is different and some are just plain stubborn and will learn when they are good and ready to learn!

Week 48

Buy some contact paper or use large sheets of heavyweight paper for art projects. Go around the house (or outside) with your baby and collect small items that can be glued to the paper. Torn pieces of colorful paper, tissue paper, old wrapping paper, feathers, and so forth are great.

Let your baby tear the paper. Let her choose the items and glue (school glue is non-toxic) them to the paper. Don't worry how this turns out. There's no right way. She may try to pull it back off. This is part of learning, so let her try. Tell her how beautiful it is.

To protect this piece of art, carefully put a piece of clear wrap over it and press down. Put her name on it, and hang it where she can see it. Another way to save it is to take pictures of it and put them in a photo album.

The magic of everyday moments—
these are the things that
grow the brain.

My Thoughts . . .   Date

_____

_____

_____

_____

_____

_____

_____

_____

_____

_____

_____

Display your baby's art no matter what it looks like. Give her the
freedom to do things her way and to be proud of her creation.
She'll gain confidence in her abilities.

Week 49

Make an indoor wagon to pull your baby around in. Find a strong cardboard box and attach a short piece of rope to one end for a handle. Give him a couple of toys, and he might even want to stay in the box for a while.

Let him pull the wagon around and use it for his own toys.

Turn the wagon on its side and roll balls into it. Show him how to do this when he's very close, and then gradually move farther away.

Paste bright pictures or paper on the box. Put his name on it in very large printed letters.

Your baby won't be ready to "share" for quite some time. Actually, he won't begin to understand that it's safe to share until he's about three years of age or older. Right now he's happy to know that things belong to him.

If you have not made another set of footprints and handprints using washable finger-paints, now is a good time. Use the next page or a blank page in the back of the book.

What is your baby's personality like? What are his favorite things to play with?

My Thoughts . . .   Date

_____

_____

_____

_____

_____

_____

_____

_____

_____

_____

_____

_____

You can put your baby's name on many things. Just make the
letters large and print them. He likes to know that things are his.
And he'll soon be able to recognize his name.

Week 50

Cardboard boxes are fun indoors and out. Find a large box to use as a playhouse. Make a couple of holes for windows and a large door so that it's easy for your baby to get in and out of it.

You can get into the "house" and use it for puppet shows. Puppets can be anything from socks to teddy bears. Play music and have the puppet sing.

Play "peek-a-boo" and "I'm going to get you." Take turns and let your baby try to get you. Slow down and let her catch you and enjoy winning this game.

Imagination games are fun and good for your baby's developing brain. Imagine the box is a house, a car, or a train. Where will you go? Who will you see? These are good questions to ask while you're driving in the car too. Eventually, your baby will learn to form "pictures" in her head. This is how she solves problems and creates new things. You can play this game for many years to help your child learn how to think.

It's such a challenge to be a good parent. Too much? Too little? Too soon? Too late? Relax, you're doing a great job.

My Thoughts . . .   **Date**

_____

_____

_____

_____

_____

_____

_____

_____

_____

_____

_____

_____

It's often hard for adults to play silly games. It's really very good for you to laugh and be silly. It's also very good for your baby.

Week 51

Get a large bucket or laundry basket and several small objects that can be dropped into it. Babies like to make a lot of noise with this.

Hold your baby or put him in his high chair and show him how to drop these things into the bucket. Let him try, and don't worry if he misses. Tell him what a great job he's doing and have fun.

Give rolled-up socks to your baby and let him throw them into the basket. These are easy for him to hold.

Rolling balls and dropping things into baskets are good for eye-hand coordination. These activities also provide a lesson in teamwork when you are playing—it's my turn, then your turn.

Babies love to throw things. When he throws something that you don't want him to, tell him no, and give him something that is okay to throw.

As your baby gets more and more independent, he will try your patience in many ways. Remember that he's really driven to learn. Many places and situations are not compatible with his needs. Most infants and toddlers just aren't designed to sit quietly for long. They're designed to explore and give their growing brains plenty of information. Make your child's needs a priority during this period of time.

Dads can be very competitive. Remind him to let your baby win sometimes.

My Thoughts . . .   Date

_____

_____

_____

_____

_____

_____

_____

_____

_____

_____

Many babies concentrate very well when they are learning new things, and are proud of their efforts. Learning new things also means making lots of mistakes. Let your baby know how proud you are that he's trying.

Week 52

Wow! Your baby is going to be one year old! A birthday party will mean more to you than to her. Find a little present to give yourself. It's hard work taking care of an infant—a big responsibility! Give yourself credit for being a good parent.

Let your baby decorate her own cake. Make or buy a simple sheet cake. Buy or make frosting. Let her do as much as possible. Nobody will care what it looks like.

Remember to take pictures as she's doing the decorating. She'll love looking back at the special time.

Playing, talking, hugging, and keeping your baby safe are important. Keep your baby safe from hurting herself and safe from people's extreme anger. She's learning at a very fast rate right now. She needs to be exposed to appropriate activities. She needs to know that it's okay to try new things and to make mistakes.

Review these activities, and use them in the next few years. Make them a little more difficult, and use your imagination.

Over the years, watch what your child seems to be interested in, and help her learn more about those things. Help her develop her natural talents and interests.

What are your hopes and dreams for your baby's future?

My Thoughts . . .   Date

_____

_____

_____

_____

_____

_____

_____

_____

_____

_____

_____

The first three years are especially important for your baby's healthy learning development. Much of your child's future will depend on these three years. Your love, patience, hugs, laughter — and your time—is just what is needed.

Creating a Learning Environment in the Upcoming Years

Your Time and Attitude

Spend as much time as you can with your child, and make it enjoyable for both of you. For many of today's parents, the most difficult challenge is finding enough time to spend with their children. "Time poverty" negatively affects the development of many children, regardless of how much money their parents have.

As baby gets more independent and needs more watching, it's often easier to try to control his activities rather than allow him to explore with his natural curiosity. Try to give baby as much opportunity to explore as possible—while keeping him safe.

Your attitude and how you treat your baby will have a big impact on how she thinks and feels about herself as an adult. Here again, the foundation is already being laid for how well she is able to express and control emotions as an adult. Be nice to your baby!

Learning takes place all of the time. Everyday activities give you an opportunity to listen, explain, or let baby try something new. We do encourage a variety of activities, just as you are encouraged to eat a variety of foods for healthy physical development.

Language

While there are debates and concerns over teaching very young children math and reading skills too early, there seems to be little disagreement about the importance of early language development.

Infant literally means "without words," but, as you've noticed, not without ways to communicate. Just as we are born with a natural desire to explore our environment, we are born with a natural desire to communicate. Our brains are, in a sense, pre-wired to talk and anxious for input.

Social skills and thinking skills develop rapidly as the ability to communicate grows. There is research showing that the number of words babies hear in the first years helps in later years to develop a larger vocabulary.

They are able to learn more words more quickly. This in turn influences social skills and reading ability.

There seems to be only one way in which we learn how to talk and that is by hearing other people talk—not through television or videos but by real people talking. We not only have to hear the words, we must also begin to understand their meaning. This takes interaction with others.

When you explain something, even if it's not understood by your child, it's an opportunity to hear words. When you say, "No you can't, because . . ." it's an opportunity to hear words. Reading provides another opportunity to hear words. You get the idea!

There is no need for drills. Having fun calls for a lot of conversation.

Math

Don't "force feed" learning activities on your young child. Formal learning such as memorizing flash cards and math problems do not enhance the type of brain growth that really makes a difference in the future.

Count everything, and have baby help. "You can put three napkins on the table, please." It's easy to introduce reading and numbers naturally in your child's everyday activities.

Reading

When reading to your child, let him join in. Point to pictures, and ask questions. Reading is often about having special time with just you. When reading time is enjoyable, your child's natural curiosity will guide this development.

And Finally . . .

Pay attention, and respect your child's talents, interests, and special personality. And, let her know how wonderful those things are.

Relax, have a great time, and give lots of hugs.

I wish you well,
Sandy Briggs

Everyone Needs a Little Help Sometimes!

Y ou'd be surprised at how many people are there to help you raise a happy and healthy child. Sometimes you just need to talk to someone; other times you need information. Local hospitals often have hot lines and offer a number of free or inexpensive classes.

Other Resources

- YMCA Child care referral services
- Free local papers for parents and families that list free activities and referrals
- Depression after Delivery—www.postpartum.net
- Child Abuse Intervention—800-4-A-Child
- Women, Infants, and Children (WIC) programs—see local telephone listing

Special Needs

If you feel your baby has some developmental problems, it's usually best to get help early. This might take some persistence and detective work on your part. A good place to start is with referral agencies like WIC and other infant health programs. You can also call your State Department of Developmental Services (or Department of Rehabilitation Services). Some agencies will offer initial assessments over the phone. New parents can be unsure about what is actual normal development. Often there is no need to worry, but follow your gut instinct. If you think there is a problem, get help for your baby.

Breastfeeding

Many parents recognize the benefits of breastfeeding, but it may be a little hard to get started. Don't give up—get some help and support. Awareness of the importance of breastfeeding is growing, as is available information. La Leche has been helping mothers for many years, as have WIC programs. Look in your area's Yellow Pages under Breast Feeding Information for phone numbers. Ask your doctor and local hospital for referrals and help.

Photographs, Keepsakes and Comments

About the Author

Many people have told Sandy that they wish they'd had the information in her book when they first became parents. She does, too! Sandy became a mother at a very young age. Her two sons were born in less than optimal circumstances. Fortunately for Sandy and her children, the grandparents embraced the family's situation and her children grew up just fine.

For many years Sandy worked with people as a career coach and became fascinated by how people learn and think, and about what motivates them. She asked herself: How do people develop a life that's satisfying and fulfilling? When research began to appear about how important an infant's formative years are to his future success, she became curious and excited. Two questions seemed to drive her as she plowed into a growing mass of research on early brain development. What do parents need to know and what do parents need to do? *Little Steps* grew out of her search for these answers.

Little Steps

Individual Quick Order Form
Little Steps for New Parents, Birth to One Year

Fax orders: 310-816-3092. Fax this form.

Telephone orders: Call 800-662-9662 (toll free)

E-mail orders: personhoodpress@att.net

Mail orders: Personhood Press, P.O. Box 1185, Torrance, CA 90505

I would like to order _____ copies of *Little Steps for New Parents* @ $15.95 each.
(For quantity discounts, special sales, and/or the Spanish version of this book,
please call our toll-free number.)

Name: _____

Address: _____

City: _____ State: _____ Zip: _____

Telephone: _____

E-mail address: _____

Sales tax: Please add 8.25% for books shipped to California addresses.

Shipping: U.S.: $5.00 for the first book and $2.00 for each additional book.

International: $9.00 for the first book and $5.00 for each additional book (estimate).

Payment: ☐ Check   Make check payable to Personhood Press.

☐ Visa   ☐ MasterCard   ☐ Discover Card   ☐ Am. Express

Card number: _____ Exp. Date: _____

Name on card: _____ Signature: _____

Please ship this as a gift to: _____

Name: _____

Address: _____

City: _____ State: _____ Zip: _____

Enclosed gift card will say, "This is a gift from _____"

Visit our website at www.personhoodpress.com

THANK YOU FOR YOUR ORDER!